Whatever happened to the Dearing Report?

UK higher education 1997–2007

David Watson

First published in 2007 by the Institute of Education, University of London
20 Bedford Way, London WC1H 0AL
www.ioe.ac.uk/publications

© Institute of Education, University of London 2007

British Library Cataloguing in Publication Data:

A catalogue record for this publication is available from the British Library

ISBN 978 0 58473 776 5

David Watson asserts the moral right to be identified as the author of this work.

Design: info@chapmandesign.net
Printed: DSI Colourworks

Institute of Education • University of London

Whatever happened to the Dearing Report?

UK higher education 1997–2007

David Watson

Professor of Higher Education Management

Based on an inaugural professorial lecture delivered at the Institute of Education,
University of London on 6 February 2007

Professor Sir David Watson

1 The 'spirit of the times'

To understand the Dearing Report you need to understand the spirit of the times. When the Committee was set up there was a real sense of crisis in UK higher education. Under the 18 years of Conservative stewardship the system had experienced:

- significant lurches of policy (from contraction to expansion and then to what was euphemistically termed 'consolidation');
- major changes in governance and organisation (from institutional stratification to radical de-stratification), and from 'national' consolidation of funding methods [the so-called ending of the 'binary line'] to territorial devolution); and, above all,
- the strains of under-funding (Watson and Bowden, 1997, 1999).

There was also a sense of paralysis within the major political parties in terms of what to do about it, not least when in the spring and summer of 1996 institutions threatened to break the mould of traditionally free higher education for full-time students by charging top-up fees. Extraordinarily, the parties then colluded in order to take the issue out of the 1997 General Election. Both front benches decided to call upon the Red Adair of educational oil-field fires, Sir Ron Dearing. His report was formally commissioned by Conservative Secretary of State, Gillian Shephard, in May 1996 and received by Labour Secretary of State, David Blunkett, on 24 July 1997. The rest is history, and it is that history which I wish to explore in this lecture.

2 The Dearing Committee

The terms of reference of the Committee were as follows.

> To make recommendations on how the purposes, shape, structure, size and funding of higher education, including support for students, should develop to meet the needs of the United Kingdom over the next twenty years, recognising that higher education embraces teaching, learning, scholarship and research.
>
> *(NICHE, 1997: 3)*

If there was more time, I would like to spend it on an *explication de texte* on this paragraph, but I am committed to continuing with the story (you can work on your own analysis while I do so).

First I should offer a few thoughts about the Committee, and how it worked. In fact it occupies a middle position, in many ways, between the Robbins Committee of 1960–61 and the White Paper of 2003 (Figure 1). The former was a research engine. The latter was the product of a highly secretive political conclave. Robbins met 151 times over a period of two and a half years. (I'll come to the contrast with the White Paper in a little while.) Robbins had set out to deal with expansion (the doubling of the size of the system in the decade of the 1960s) before it happened. Dearing was invited to do the same, after the event (the further doubling in size of the system between the mid-1980s and early 1990s).

There were 18 members of the Committee: purportedly 'balanced' in terms of institutional affiliation, experience, age and gender (see Appendix I). We worked for almost exactly a calendar year. There were 21 Main Committee meetings between 21 May 1996 and 24 July 1997, although the first serious working meeting was the third (on 27 June 1996) and the report itself was approved at the twentieth (on 26 June 1997). A separate Scottish Committee was established in June 1996, and reported on the same time-scale.

Individual members had their *idées fixes* – like two-year degrees, regional priorities, skills for employment, the technological fix, and concentration of

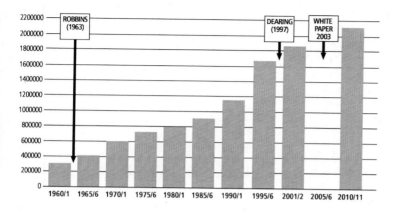

Figure 1 Total higher education student numbers, UK 1960/01–2010/11

Source: DES 1969; HESA 1999; 2002; HEPI 2003

Figure 2 Members of the Dearing Committee

3

research funding. However, the overwhelming commitment was towards working 'with the grain' of what was regarded as high-performing and already impressively diverse system. Individuals did come with strong personal views and commitments and did change their minds in the face of evidence and others' opinions. At the end of the day, we agreed on the big things, and with good will.

We worked very much in public, through consultative processes and questionnaires. We looked at developments elsewhere in the world (with visits to Japan, Holland, the United States [twice], Germany, France, Australia, New Zealand and Malaysia). We published all of our commissioned working papers. We held hearings, and each piece of written evidence submitted (there were over 6,000 pages in total) was read in detail and reported on by at least two members of the Committee (NCIHE, 1997: Chapter 2). As a Chairman, Ron Dearing was a hard taskmaster. He divided us up, gave us jobs, and whenever anyone expressed a strong opinion he or she found that there was a paper to write. As a consequence, a wide variety of views, and many other people (several of whom later found it convenient to forget this) had their day in court.

I have spent the last year intermittently working through my personal archive (which I have donated to the Institute of Education). An amazing amount of work was done and with significant attention to detail. That is not to say the Committee failed to play its major cards close to its chest: you could in fact have anticipated almost all of the key themes by taking the front page of the *THES* and reversing the meaning of their headlines about what we were going to say (examples were 'a research super-league', 'US-style community colleges', and 'two-year degrees for all').

3 The Report

At the end of the day, the main report was nearly 500 pages; the total number of pages (including appendices) was over 2,000 (Figure 3). The boxed set weighed 2.2 kg, and one reviewer claims to have broken a bone in his foot when he dropped it. It made 93 recommendations, brutally summarised here. If we had had more time we would either have got up to 100, or written a shorter report.

Key messages in the Dearing Report

- Endorsement of a return to expansion, especially at the higher national certificate and diploma levels.
- Concern to protect the standing of UK degrees, leading to strong strictures on system-wide quality and standards.
- Greater use of communications and information technology.
- A warning against cutting short-term funding.
- Enhanced professionalism in teaching.
- New funding for research.
- Full-time students to contribute approx. £1,000 per annum after graduation on an income-contingent basis (plus return of means-tested maintenance grants).
- Stronger regional and community role for higher education.
- A review of pay and working practices.

Figure 3 The full Dearing Report

The full list of recommendations is in Appendix II. For many reasons, the fate of these has been variable. Leaving aside funding, and student support (see recommendations 68–83), to which I shall return, I think we can discern the following lines of development.

Some recommendations were clearly 'of their time', in particular in relation to organisational structures (84–93). 'Devolution' of responsibility for higher education – strongly to the Scottish Parliament, weakly to the Welsh assembly, and intermittently to Stormont – overtook many of these.

Some were necessarily 'slow release' and took a long time.

- The review of pay rates and structures (following the Bett review [Bett, 1999]) is the classic here, with full implementation only from September 2006 (50).
- 'Progress Files' (and the review of degree classifications) limp along, now under the aegis of the Burgess Group (20) (UUK/SCOP, 2004). The same is true of credit and the 'national qualifications framework' (22).
- Admissions policies and procedures remain contentious (and not really moved forward by the Schwartz Review [DfES, 2004]); post-qualifications admissions (PQA) are still being debated (10, 17).
- We continue to agonise over how to improve the role of business and industry as 'intelligent customers' of HE goods and services, including following the Lambert Review (30, 37) (Lambert, 2003).
- We are closer to full indirect costs of research contracts as a result of TRAC and Full Economic Costing (FEC), although there are still strains (34, 52).
- At the same time, ideas about an Industrial Development Partnership Fund have borne fruit in formula and competitive funding for '3rd leg' activity and other elements of the *Science & Innovation Strategy, 2004–14* (34) (HMT/DTI/DfES, 2004).

Some were simply overtaken by events.

- The Institute for Learning and Teaching in Higher Education (ILTHE) has come and gone (13,14, 48), and is now absorbed into the Higher Education Academy (HEA).
- Many of the ideas about networking and the use of ICT in HE have taken different, but equally effective routes (44, 45).
- Foundation degrees were not anticipated (and indeed two-year associate degrees were specifically ruled out); there was no thought of degree-awarding powers for FE colleges (67).

A few received raspberries.

- The classic here was the suggestion that institutions could opt out of the Research Assessment Exercise (RAE) in return for a level of non-competitive funding of research (34). (A similar idea proposed in the Roberts Review of Research Assessment in 2003 met the same fate [HEFCE, 2003].)
- Another was the suggestion that all new entrants to the profession should join the Universities Superannuation Scheme (USS) (51).
- The Committee was keen on tightening rather than loosening the criteria for 'university' and 'university college' status (62–66).
- Perhaps most controversial was the suggestion that under certain circumstances degree-awarding powers could be removed (64).

But many of the core ideas have, I think resonated with the sector at its best, and have made a difference. These include:

- the priority of funding widening participation (2–6, 12);
- the enhancement of learning and teaching , and related staff development (8, 9);
- the value of work experience (18, 19);

- the irreducible responsibility of institutions for making awards, including through 'franchised' arrangements (23), linked with the central role of the Quality Assurance Agency (QAA) (24) (including on 'benchmarking [24]);
- formalising the process for making complaints (as has now arrived with the Office of the Independent Adjudicator [OIA] [25, 60]);
- the establishment of the Arts and Humanities Research Council (AHRC) (29);
- actions to improve the effectiveness of university governance (55–59);
- better information for intending students (85); and, a recommendation that has been forgotten by many of the critics of Dearing's apparent 'instrumentalism';
- taking steps to ensure the breadth as well as the depth of programmes of study (16).

In our book, *Lifelong Learning and the University: a post-Dearing agenda* (published in 1998), Dick Taylor and I suggested that there were at least four sets of animating ideas in the Report as a whole.

- The first was the contribution of higher education to lifelong learning, as embedded particularly in the qualifications framework, views on articulation and collaboration between education sectors, and especially fairer and more effective support for all types of learners in HE.
- The second involved a vision for learning in the twenty-first century, as embodied in ideas about credit and the qualifications framework, assurance of standards as well as quality, teacher professionalism, Communication & Information Technology (C&IT), key skills, and work experience.
- Funding research according to its intended outcomes came

third, as set out in a multi-stranded model for research evaluation and funding; leading to rejection of the notion of a 'teaching-only' university.

- The final big idea was that of the 'compact', essentially a 'deal' (David Blunkett referred explicitly to a 'new deal' in responding to the Report in Parliament) whereby institutions retain their independence and gain increased security in return for clearer accountability (especially on standards) and greater responsiveness to a wide range of legitimate stakeholders (Watson and Taylor, 1998: 151–2).

The Report delineated what it called a 'new compact' in some detail, as summarised in Appendix III.

With the benefit of hindsight, there was a number of issues which the Committee missed, did not have time fully to probe, or simply got wrong. Some of these were as follows.

- We miscalculated the costs of full implementation of the ideas in the report about quality assurance, and external examiners.
- The recommendations on student computing (46) fell between the two stools of university provision of networked terminals and student ownership.
- We 'side-lined' teacher education to a separate report (by Stuart Sutherland) that basically reaffirmed the *status quo* (NCIHE, 1997: Report 10).
- We didn't get inside issues related to loans for part-time students and failed accurately to establish the position of support for such students by employers.
- We could have done much more on the global context of higher education and, in particular, on the challenges of internationalism.
- Above all, as suggested above, we failed to spot impending

devolution. The relative freedom given to the Scottish Committee meant that some issues (for example about length of courses, about the framework for qualifications, and about cross-border flows) could have been better understood and resolved before relevant powers were devolved.

- We sensibly decided to stand aside from the vexed contemporary question of Oxford and Cambridge College fees.

4 Reactions

The Dearing Committee was accused by a number of commentators of 'lacking vision'. In most instances they simply meant that it lacked *their* vision. Perhaps the most trenchant such attack came from a predictable source: Martin Trow, whom the Committee had entertained to lunch in June 1996. In the *THES* in October 1997 his attack was personal: he described the 'shocking ignorance' of the academic members about how their institutions actually work and of the 'private life' of such institutions. A different sort of visitor was Lord Claus Moser – himself a vital link back to the work of Robbins – who was consistently encouraging

More generally, a sort of lazy critique has subsequently developed in which the Committee is accused (I am convinced by commentators who have not actually read the Report – and almost certainly not its chapter on teaching and learning) of a kind of naïve instrumentalism. Examples are Alison Wolf, Mary Evans and Stephen Rowland (Wolf, 2003: 225, 290; Evans, 2004: 22; and Rowland, 2006: 9, 52). To take just one example: in the course of Evans' celebrated critique of quality assurance we are told that the Dearing Report 'explicitly stated that universities had four functions: they should be a significant force in the regional economy, support research and consultancy and attract inward investment, provide new employment and meet labour market needs and foster entrepreneurship among students and staff'. This is, in fact, a quotation from Dearing's chapter on the regional economic role of universities (NICHE, 1997: Chapter 10).

Dearing's actual 'four purposes of higher education' are as follows (and worth quoting in full).

- To inspire and enable individuals to develop their capabilities to the highest potential levels throughout life, so that they grow intellectually, are well-equipped for work, can contribute effectively to society and achieve personal fulfilment.
- To increase knowledge and understanding for its own sake and to foster their application to the benefit of the economy and society.
- To serve the needs of an adaptable, sustainable, knowledge-based economy at local, regional and national levels.
- To play a major role in shaping a democratic, civilized, inclusive society (this last one is I think a significant step on from Robbins' appeal to a 'common culture') (NCIHE, 1997: Chapter 5).

5 Politics: New Labour and Dearing

So what actually happened? I do have to begin with the politics (see Watson 2006a).

New Labour's first term policy on higher education (New Labour Mark I) was structured around Dearing, with the exception of a serious modification of his recommendations on fees and student support, which has haunted them ever since. Essentially, the government was too greedy. Ministers took the Dearing recommendation of a student contribution to course costs and ignored what the report said about living costs, especially for poorer students. Simultaneously, they completed a Conservative project of turning all student grants into loans (Gillian Shephard in fact sold the loan book, while the Committee was working, in September 1996). This precipitate decision has

become the Achilles heel of subsequent New Labour policy for higher education. Almost every major policy initiative, and certainly every discussion
of how the system should be funded overall, has been drawn back into a kind
of *maelstrom* of misunderstanding, of posturing and of bad faith about costs
and charges to students, exacerbated by an aggrieved middle-class sense of
entitlement.

The new government was, of course, almost immediately forced to trim: the
student fee became means-tested (in 2005–06 – the last year of the old regime
– only about 40 per cent of students paid the full fee), but at the expense of
immense bureaucracy and transaction costs; hardship funds were distributed
via universities (but only after all loan facilities were taken up). Initially these
were called 'access' funds because ministers had difficulty with the concept of
'hardship;' and 'specific' grants were progressively added to the mix (with the
usual problem: the more precisely you set conditions for a benefit, the less
likely it is to be taken up). Meanwhile, post-devolution Scotland decided to go
a different way (rejecting up-front fees); and Wales would like to (although
can't apparently afford to).

As I have suggested, much else in the Dearing Report, *Higher Education in
the Learning Society* (NCIHE, 1997), has come to pass, although not always
exactly as intended (see Watson and Bowden, 2000). The government
followed the Committee in devising a policy essentially 'with the grain' of a
formally unstratified system and it reached its height in 2000 with David
Blunkett's speech at Greenwich on 'Modernising Higher Education: meeting
the global challenge'. New Labour Mark I recognised that the achievements of
the sector as a whole depended on the nurturing of different types of institution with different missions, but fundamentally within sector-wide
arrangements: for quality assurance, for funding, and for fair competition
(including for research support). It resisted strong calls to 'put the polytech-
nics back in their box', and subsequent performance suggests that this was
right (Watson and Bowden, 2002). Indeed one of the problems with the Blunkett speech was that it insisted on a universal agenda, that each institution
should 'all do it all' (Watson, 2002).

David Blunkett's agenda for HEIs

- Balance teaching, research and knowledge transfer.
- Secure improved quality across each of these missions.
- Support wider participation and the drive for social inclusion.
- Expand into new markets.
- Preserve and enhance the sector's 'traditional scholarship role'.
- Improve management capacity.
- Staff development.
- Accountability to government and society.
- Links with employers and others.
- Careers guidance and work placements.
- Utilise information and communication technologies (ICT) more systematically and effectively.
- And, not least, tackle the unacceptable situation in terms of equal opportunities.

(Based on Blunkett, 2000: 30)

The change of emphasis was sudden, and caught many supporters by surprise. The country had, for example, been in serious 'read my lips mode' about the unacceptability of differential fees until well into the second term. The shunt arose from remarks by the Prime Minister, added at the last minute to his Labour Party conference speech in Brighton in September 2001, that there would be a review of student support. What emerged eventually was a much more comprehensive U-turn.

One of the main intentions of the 2003 White Paper, *The future of higher education* (Figure 4), the 2004 Higher Education Act, and subsequent announcements (otherwise New Labour Mark II), appears to be the re-emergence of a re-stratified system, endorsed at the highest level. These proposals emerged from the DfES after a period of drafting and re-drafting – entirely in secret, and by civil servants (supported by the Funding Council) – which lasted longer, at fourteen months, than the entire Dearing exercise. New

Figure 4 The 2003 White Paper, *The future of higher education*

Labour apparently wants to put the clock back. Collectively the proposals:

- replace a flat-rate system of student fees, with a 'variable' or 'top-up' regime;
- herald even greater concentration of public funding of research;
- begin to categorise institutions, as for example, 'research-intensive', or 'more focused on teaching and learning', or 'engaged in serving local and regional economies';
- dilute the controlled reputational range of UK universities by lowering the bar for university title and admitting new entrants to both university status, including a 'for profit' sector.

The Dearing Committee had anticipated variable fees as a likely development, but stressed the Committee's 'principal concern with the well-being of the whole sector rather than that of individual institutions' (NCIHE, 1997: 301).

2003 White Paper main themes

- Six per cent increase in base-line funding, but heavily ear-marked.

- Deregulation of fees (between £0 and £3,000) from 2006, 'graduate contribution scheme', restoration of grants and grants for part-timers.
- 'Access agreements' and regulator (Office for Fair Access [OFFA]).
- Concentration of 'R' funding, Knowledge Exchanges, Centres for Excellence in Teaching and Learning (CETLs).
- University status possible on undergraduate degree-awarding powers only.
- New Arts and Humanities Research Council (AHRC).
- Accreditation of teachers, the Academy for the Advancement of Learning and Teaching in Higher Education, and the Leadership Foundation.
- Expansion principally through Foundation Degrees.
- National survey of student views and published external examiners reports.

(DfES, 2003)

The result, in January 2004, was one of the most compelling Commons battles of the Parliament (the anticipated show-down in the Lords, where much of the action on the preceding Conservative government's HE bills had taken place was, in contrast, a damp squib). The Prime Minister's reputation was on the line; concessions were made up to the last minute of the second reading debate in January 2004; the vote was extremely tight (a majority of five); and the result was a compromise which has been widely (and accurately) reported as really satisfying no one.

The new 'maximum' fee of £3,000 has turned out in effect to be a revised flat-rate fee, with very few institutions charging less (notably Leeds Metropolitan and Greenwich) and none, so far, zero. Indeed by setting a low limit (evidence released under the Freedom of Information act suggests that sums up to £5,000 were mooted) and a very high Parliamentary hurdle for its upwards revision (positive resolution by both Houses), it is hard to see that much has changed: except for the Exchequer, which will have to fund the institutions in advance of earning back the 'graduate contribution' (this is undoubtedly why ministers have so far failed fully to follow through on a commitment to extend the deferral elements of the scheme to part-time students). Certainly those expecting the 'cap' simply to disappear following a planned review in 2009–10 have underestimated the obstacles: not only the Parliamentary hurdle and Treasury nervousness, but also political will in general in this contentious area. In the meantime, this modest adjustment to what the Department euphemistically calls 'publicly planned funding' is accompanied by a huge paraphernalia of 'reviews', of transaction costs, and of regulation (notably the Office for Fair Access [OFFA], whose teeth – much talked up in the debate – have apparently been drawn).

The government wanted a 'market' and it now has one, but not where it was planned. Fees are not only almost uniform, but have the significant merit of being deferred (with income-contingent repayment after graduation). The serious competition will be over bursaries and other incentives, without much positive impact on widening participation. The most socially progressive institutions will feel obliged to re-cycle the greatest proportion of their additional fee income to needy students, while most of the relevant action will be about well-qualified students from clued-up families operating their own 'post-qualifications auctions'.

The brutal conclusion of an analysis of New Labour's record to date is about the failure of public funding (Watson and Bowden, 2005), most notably in support of teaching. Here is the long, sorry story of the 'unit of resource' (Table 1). This is the element of the 'compact' which, perhaps predictably, has been most conspicuously lacking.

Table 1 Unit of public funding of teaching, 1979–2005

YEAR	UNIVERSITY	INDEX HEFCE	POLYTECHNIC
1979/80	100		100
1980/81	106		99
1981/82	103		94
1982/83	106		89
1983/84	107		82
1984/85	106		79
1985/86	103		78
1986/87	102		79
1987/88	105		76
1988/89	103		75
1989/90	100	100	–
1990/91		91	
1991/92		86	
1992/93		80	
1993/94		75	
1994/95		73	
1995/96		70	
1996/97		65	
1997/98		64	
1998/99		63	
1999/2000		63	
2000/01		62	
2001/02		63	
2002/03		59	
2003/04		61	
2004/05		61	
2005/06		63	

Sources: CVCP (1995); UUK (2003)

More broadly, Dearing did not stimulate a revival of investment, except in the highly significant area of infrastructural support for scientific research (and because of conditions about 'matching funding' there were also negative unintended consequences here). Public funding of higher education (including of student support) as a proportion of gross domestic product (GDP) remains in the bottom third of the OECD league, well behind our main competitors. It has also fallen significantly behind investment in other educational sectors.

Table 2 Department for Education and Skills resource budget, 2001–2006

	2001/02 outturn	2005/06 plans	% change 01/02 – 05/06 (cash terms)
Schools, including Sixth Forms	£3,491m	£6,899m	98%
Higher Education	£6,006m	£8,142m	36%
Further Education, Adult Learning and Skills and Lifelong Learning	£5,815m	£8,452m	45%
Total DfES Resource Budget	£23,844m	£34,129m	43%

Source: Watson and Bowden, 2005: 33

Meanwhile some parts of the sector may be close to financial melt-down. The latest HEFCE summary of institutions' financial forecasts shows that the operating position of the sector will fall from a surplus of about 1.0 per cent in 2004–05 to a deficit of 0.4 per cent in 2005–06 (HEFCE, 2006). It is becoming clear that a substantial minority of institutions are running accumulated deficits on the basis that additional fee income from 2006–07 onwards will simply back-fill these rather than be available for the improvements students (as paying customers) will expect to see.

The temptation is to conclude that not much has changed; a 'traditional' system has simply got larger and less financially secure. There is also a sense that progress in key areas – including many of those which relate to equity – slowed during the last Parliament.

It is also relevant that the Parliament of 2001–05 was an even more than usually feverish one: with the response to international terrorism, the war in Iraq, foundation hospitals, and the ban on hunting with dogs, to say nothing of the breakdown of the ideological 'marriage' at the heart of the government. New Labour's first Parliament had one Secretary of State for Education and Skills. Its second had three. Probably the most impressive was Charles Clarke, but even he betrayed the lack of a corporate memory about higher education policy by sending out his own quick-response 'consultation paper' (a technique for thinking time borrowed from one of his Conservative predecessors, Gillian Shephard). Within other countries the notion of all bets being off in terms of the direction of major public services, not just when governments change but when new ministers arrive and have to 'read themselves' into the job, would seem extraordinary. Certainly, it indicates little confidence in an ongoing compact.

At the time of writing, there is a sense of both exhaustion and irritation in New Labour's third term in office. The key politicians would like higher education to revert to being 'finished business'.

Meanwhile, there are clues about future directions for New Labour. We have a White Paper on Further Education (*Further Education: raising skills, improving life chances*) that has put Level 3 achievement back at the top of the agenda, supported now by Lord Leitch's suggestion (long overdue) that education and/or training should be required at least up to the age of 18 (Leitch, 2006: 4). The 2006 budget further consolidated the 'Science and Innovation Framework', by ring-fencing medical research funding across Whitehall and holding out the prospect of a post-RAE, metrics-driven system of institutional funding for research. The Further Education Bill, currently before Parliament holds out the prospect of degree-awarding powers for Foundation degrees for FE Colleges. And, finally, there is the commitment to a review in 2009–10 of the new funding and student support arrangements.

The story I have told demonstrates how expectations of a 'compact' between higher education and the state have foundered on a reef of political cynicism and academic unrealism. The outcome is a kind of cautionary tale. New Labour inherited a massively expanded system of HE, and has (with the exception of selective investment in science) not really transformed it any serious way. They remain trapped in traditional dilemmas about funding and organisation (where the politicians would like mission differentiation while institutions chase similar measures of esteem). They have potentially created a monster in the model chosen for the 'graduate contribution', and certainly placed an unintended constraint on further equity through expansion (as well as on achieving their much-vaunted target of 50 per cent of each age cohort participating in HE). Widening participation has stalled (Watson, 2006b). Above all, perhaps, in their obsession with the 'world-class' status of a very few institutions they have taken their eye off the ball of what the Dearing 'compact' really meant: the aim of a world-class sector of higher education, fit for the challenges of the twenty-first century (Watson, 2006).

In 1997 there was a real sense of a political era coming to an end. The Major-Thatcher era had run out of steam. Can we speculate in similar fashion about Blair-Brown? Much of the running on HE today seems to be being made by Willetts-Johnson.

6 Inside the sector: before and after Dearing

This has been a largely political account of a politically commissioned report. As Ron Dearing comments: 'our objective was to have a report ready for whatever government was elected, so that there were financial options for immediate decision' (private communication). And politicians do very significantly make the weather for universities, at least in the UK. There are, however, other very important threads to the story, including, critically, what I would call the 'inner game' of higher education. Here the story is more optimistic.

So what effect did the post-Dearing reforms actually have? At the macro-level, it is clear that some elements of the system continued inexorably, before during and after Dearing. These include growth and diversity. They are best shown, I think, by looking at student enrolments, by level and type of course, as in Figure 5.

Understanding other aspects of the performance of the system has been

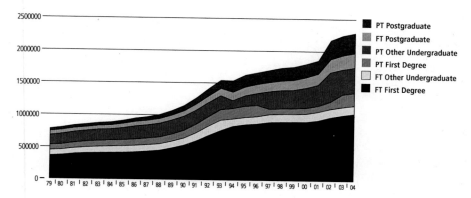

Figure 5 UK student enrolment by level and type of course

Source: HESA Red Books on student numbers

made easier and more disciplined by the series of reports now produced annually by the Longer Term Strategy Group of UUK: the *Patterns* series (of which the sixth was published in September 2006). In many cases, we can now see trends over a full decade. Here are some examples.

First is the pattern of student enrolments, reflecting the ways in which the 'market' has continued to mould the system. Here the interesting contrast is between two sorts of rapid growth: a supply-side investment in health-related courses, and a demand side boom in 'media studies' (Figure 6).

The market, of course is not just for subjects, but also for courses by mode and level. Here the key developments are above average growth in part-time undergraduate and full-time postgraduate enrolments (Table 3).

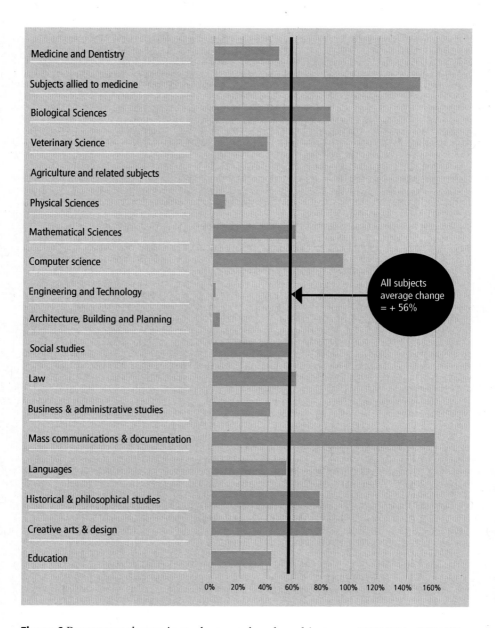

Figure 6 Percentage change in student numbers by subject area, 1995/96 to 2004/05

Source: UUK, 2006: Figure 1

Table 3 Percentage change in student numbers by mode and level 1995/96 to 2004/05

	United Kingdom %	England %	Wales %	Scotland %	Northern Ireland %
POSTGRADUATES					
1995/96 to 2004/05	43.9	45.6	45.3	32.6	31.2
2003/04 to 2004/05	1.7	1.7	1.0	2.4	−0.3
UNDERGRADUATES					
1995/96 to 2004/05	30.0	28.1	41.6	37.6	43.7
2003/04 to 2005/05	1.8	1.4	5.0	2.7	5.2
All students					
1995/96 to 2004/05	33.0	31.8	42.3	36.4	40.8
2003/04 to 2004/05	1.8	1.5	4.2	2.7	4.0
CHANGE IN PART-TIME NUMBERS					
POSTGRADUATES					
1995/96 to 2004/05	30.6	30.7	49.0	22.9	27.6
2003/04 to 2004/05	1.0	1.3	0.8	−0.7	−1.6
UNDERGRADUATES					
1995/96 to 2004/05	56.2	47.4	135.7	179.6	72.6
2003/04 to 2005/05	1.3	0.0	9.6	11.3	8.0
CHANGE IN FULL-TIME NUMBERS					
POSTGRADUATES					
1995/96 to 2004/05	67.0	71.9	40.5	48.2	38.1
2003/04 to 2004/05	2.6	2.2	1.3	6.6	2.2
UNDERGRADUATES					
1995/96 to 2004/05	19.8	19.8	13.7	20.3	35.3
2003/04 to 2005/05	2.1	2.2	2.4	0.6	4.3

Source: UUK, 2006: Table 4

David Watson

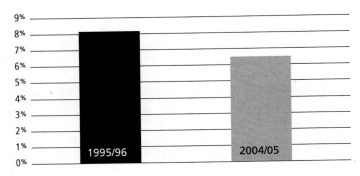

Figure 7 Unemployment rate of full-time first degree UK graduates

Source: UUK, 2006: Figure 15

What about 'employability' (an associated question is about so-called 'under-employment)? The system continues to perform strongly (Figure 7), as is acknowledged by Leitch, who would like to see the proportion of the workforce with graduate level qualifications rise to 40 per cent by 2020 (Leitch, 2006: 137).

Finally a snap-shot on where students live (Figure 8). Are we becoming, slowly, more like our continental neighbours?

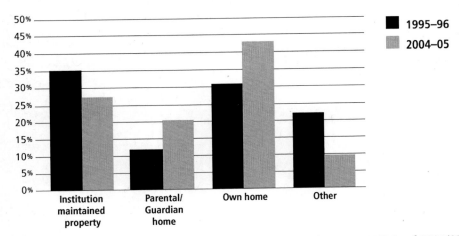

Figure 8 Term-time accommodation of full-time undergraduates, 1995/96 and 2004/05

Source: UUK, 2006: Figure 12

7 Facing the future

From data like this we can generate a number of questions about the potential futures for UK higher education.

- How can it solve its economic problems?
- Will it contribute to social justice, or the reverse?
- Will it enable the UK to enhance its position in a global knowledge economy?
- Will it continue to supply satisfying experiences to its members, and former members?

Underlying questions like this one is, I think a prior question, which lies at the heart of the Dearing Report and its legacy. Will there continue to be a recognisable sector of higher education, in the sense that – at a moral as well as a practical level – the members exercise a degree of responsibility for each other and for the whole (what I have called elsewhere a 'controlled reputational range' [Watson, 2002])? One of the most distinctive features of the development of the UK system of higher education has been its willingness to take academic responsibility for its own enlargement.

The UK system is admired around the world for its commitment to systematic peer review. So it is deeply ironic that at home the 'quality wars' have threatened to tear the *sector* apart. If you take the long historical view, the 'collaborative' gene was there from the start, for example through London external degrees and the system of 'validating universities' (notably the Victoria University of Manchester). External members of university college committees played their part in the late nineteenth and early twentieth centuries, before the two major phases of late twentieth-century expansion. These were overseen, in turn, by 'academic advisory committees' for the post-Robbins foundations and by the Council for National Academic Awards (CNAA) for what was termed 'public sector higher education'. But perhaps the most potent symbol is that of the 'external examiner', a figure of immense moral importance, significantly envied in other systems.

Following the Conservative legislation of 1988 and 1992, some of these functions were indeed bureaucratised, and the sector tried – late in the day – to take pre-emptive action against the encroachment of the state. But the paradox was that, as the world beat a path to the UK door to learn about how to do some of these things, a series of 'popular revolts' at home did their best to do away with them.

There is serious work to be done on quality assurance: to bring up to date the internationally respected system of external examination; to identify and control for the issues raised by innovations in teaching and learning, and especially in student assessment; to probe the deeper issues raised by the relationship between teaching and research; to take steps to ensure that collaborative provision between institutions – sometimes across wide distances, and making use of new media – lives up to its intentions on quality and standards; to calibrate external interventions so that they are led by secure assessment of risk and not just reputation; to think hard about acceptable standards of advertising and promotion; and so on. To achieve these things will require imagination; it will require trust and mutual respect; and it will require going with the grain of an academic community operating at its best. Is it too late? (See Watson, 2006c.)

It is in this context that the Dearing Report's approach to institutional diversity needs to be understood, and often hasn't been (on 17 October 1997 the *THES* had a headline: 'Diversity: big issue Dearing ducked'). This is what the Report in fact said:

> The diversity of programme provision and of students will continue to be a valued element in higher education…. However, we seek to encourage diversity within a framework where qualifications are widely understood, standards are high and respected, and the quality of teaching and student support is amongst the best in the world.
>
> *(NICHE, 1997: 10.102; see also Watson 1999)*

This why it is important to recognise that even the most powerful institution can't really go it alone. At some stage, and for some important purposes, every institution is going to rely on the strength and reputation of the system as a whole. The dialectic between competition, collaboration, and complementarity in HE is a complex one. Mike Boxall, from PA Consulting, has likened it to the *peleton* in a cycle race. This is a good metaphor. Individuals do come out of the pack, to compete for various prizes ('king of the mountains', 'points' for sprinting, etc.). There's also the *poubelle* (dustbin) bringing up the rear. But inside the *peleton* itself there is *esprit de corps* and unwritten rules (leading through your home town, assisting in re-grouping after crashes, etc.). Members of teams work for each other (including *domestiques*). Meanwhile the race remains a competition, including simply to finish: they *could* all ride slower.

8 Dearing 2018?

The editors of a recent collection of essays on *Taking Public Universities Seriously* identify three big questions, with resonance all around the world. These are about:

- assessing public and private benefits in the context of 'who should pay?';
- testing the priority, in a competitive and stretched world, of government investment in higher education;
- and weighing the 'appropriate balance between centralisation and decentralisation in the governance of the public university sector'.

These were the same questions as given to Dearing. How do these questions fit together? The notion at the heart of this discourse of a 'compact' between universities and the communities they serve on the one hand, and the state on the other, is apparently almost universally seductive (Iacobucci and Touhy, 2005: xi–xix). It could be said that the Dearing Committee tested the idea of a higher education compact to destruction.

In these circumstances, should we do it again? Is another Dearing Committee indicated? Recommendation 88 was that there should be a 'review of higher education in 5 years' time and subsequently every 10 years'. In July 2007 the Centre for Higher Education Studies (CHES) at the Institute of Education will host a conference on 'the Dearing Report – ten years on'. Not wishing to pre-empt those discussions, I am not convinced that another major Commission would help in finding new answers to old questions. Unfashionably, I think we have had too much higher education policy-making in the heroic style. What I would like the politicians and the institutions to do today is to relax; to recognise what is unfinished business, in the medium as well as the short term; to invest sufficiently to stabilise what is a very highly performing sector, so that it can restore its collaborative gene and do good work.

References

Bett, Sir M. (1999) *Independent Review of Higher Education Pay and Conditions.* London: HMSO.

Blunkett, D. (2000) *Modernising Higher Education: facing the global challenge.* Speech at the University of Greenwich, 15 February. London: DfEE.

Department for Education and Skills (DfES) (2003) *The Future of Higher Education,* White Paper, Cmnd 5735. Norwich: The Stationery Office.

Department for Education and Skills (DfES) (2004) *Fair Admissions to Higher Education.* London: DfES.

Evans, M. (2004) *Killing Thinking: The death of the universities.* London and New York: Continuum.

H. M. Treasury (HMT), Department of Trade and Industry (DTI), Department for Education and Skills (DfES) (2004) *Science and Innovation Investment Framework 2004–2014.* London: The Stationery Office.

Higher Education Funding Council for England (HEFCE) (2003) *Joint Consultation on the Review of Research Assessment.* Bristol: HEFCE.

Higher Education Funding Council for England (HEFCE) (2006) *Initial analysis of 2006 financial forecasts.* Bristol: HEFCE (14 December).

Iacobucci, F. and Tuohy, C. (eds) (2005) *Taking Public Universities Seriously,* Toronto: University of Toronto Press.

Lambert, R. (2003) *Lambert Review of University-Business Collaboration.* Norwich: HMSO (December).

Leitch Review of Skills (2006) *Prosperity for All in the Global Economy – world class skills.* London: HM Treasury.

National Committee of Inquiry into Higher Education (NICHE) (1997) *Higher Education in the Learning Society* (the Dearing Report) London: HMSO.

Rowland, S. (2006) *The Enquiring University: Compliance and contestation in higher education.* Maidenhead: Open University Press.

Trow, M. (1997) 'More trouble than it's worth'. *Times Higher Education Supplement,* 24 October.

Universities UK (UUK) (2006) *Patterns of UK Higher Education Institutions: The sixth report.* London: UUK.

Universities UK (UUK) and Standing Conference of Principals (SCOP) (2004) *Measuring and Recording Student Achievement.* London: UUK and SCOP.

Watson, D. (1999) 'Decoding Dearing on Diversity'. In Mary Henkel and Brenda Little (eds) *Changing Relationships between Higher Education and the State,* 325–37. London: Jessica Kingsley.

Watson, D. (2002) 'Can we all do it all? Tensions in the structure and mission of UK higher education'. *Higher Education Quarterly,* 56: 2 (April), 143–55.

Watson, D. (2006a) 'New Labour and Higher Education'. *Perspectives – policy and practice in higher education.* Part I, in volume 10: 3 (July 2006), 63–8. Part two in volume 10: 4 (November 2006), 92–6.

Watson, D. (2006b) *How to Think about Widening Participation.* Report for the Higher Education Funding Council for England (HEFCE). July. Available online. http://www.hefce.ac.uk/pubs/rdreports/2006/rd13_06/

Watson, D. (2006c) *Who Killed What in the Quality Wars?* Gloucester: Quality Assurance Agency for Higher Education (QAA).

Watson, D. and Bowden, R. (1997) *Ends Without Means: The Conservative stewardship of UK higher education, 1979–1997,* University of Brighton Education Research Centre Occasional Paper. University of Brighton, April.

Watson, D. and Bowden, R. (1999) 'Why did they do it? The Conservatives and mass higher education'. *Journal of Education Policy* 14:3, 243–56.

Watson, D. and Bowden, R. (2000) *After Dearing: A mid-term report.* University of Brighton Education Research Centre Occasional Paper. University of Brighton, July.

Watson, D. and Bowden, R. (2001) *Can We Be Equal and Excellent Too? The New Labour stewardship of UK higher education, 1997–2001.* University of Brighton Education Research Centre Occasional Paper. University of Brighton, June.

Watson, D. and Bowden, R. (2002) *The New University Decade, 1992–2002.* University of Brighton Education Research Centre Occasional Paper. University of Brighton, September.

Watson, D. and Bowden, R. (2005) *The Turtle and the Fruit Fly: New Labour and UK higher education, 2001–2005.* University of Brighton Education Research Centre Occasional Paper. University of Brighton, May.

Watson, D. and Taylor, R. (1998) *Lifelong Learning and the University: A post-Dearing agenda.* London: Falmer Press.

Wolf, Alison (2003) *Does Education Matter? Myths about education and economic growth.* London: Penguin.

Appendix I: Members of the Dearing Committee (positions at the time)

Professor John Arbuthnott	Principal and Vice-Chancellor of the University of Strathclyde
Baroness Dean of Thornton-le-Fylde	(formerly Brenda Dean)
Sir Ron Dearing	(Chairman)
Ms Judith Evans	Departmental Director of Personnel Policy, Sainsbury's
Sir Ron Garrick	Managing Director and Chief Executive of Weir Group
Sir Geoffrey Holland	Vice-Chancellor of the University of Exeter
Professor Diana Laurillard	Pro Vice-Chancellor (Technology Development) of the Open University
Mrs Pamela Morris	Headteacher, The Blue School, Wells
Sir Ronald Oxburgh	Rector of Imperial College of Science, Technology and Medicine
Dr David Potter	Chairman of Psion plc
Sir George Quigley	Chairman of Ulster Bank
Sir William Stubbs	Rector of the London Institute
Sir Richard Sykes	Chairman and Chief Executive of Glaxo Wellcome plc
Professor David Watson	Director of the University of Brighton
Professor Sir David Weatherall	Regius Professor of Medicine at the University of Oxford

Professor Adrian Webb	Vice-Chancellor of the University of Glamorgan
Mr Simon Wright	Education and Welfare Officer, Students Union, the University of Wales College of Cardiff

Secretary to the National Committee

Mrs Shirley Trundle	Department for Education and Employment

Appendix II: Dearing Committee recommendations

R1   Lift cap on full-time undergraduate places.
     Lift cap on full-time sub-degree places.

R2   Priority in funding expansion to institutions committed to widening participation.

R3   Collaborate and fund projects to promote progression to higher education.

R4   Funding Bodies to consider financing pilot projects to enrol students from disadvantaged localities.

R5   • Consider restoring social security benefits to full-time students.
     • Double and extend scope of Access funds.

R6   Improved learning support for students with disabilities. Extend scope of Disabled Student Allowance.

R7   Creation of data framework for lifelong learning.

R8   Develop and implement learning and teaching strategies.

R9   Review changing role of staff as a result of Communications and IT (C&IT) and ensure training and support for staff and students.

R10 Establish a post-qualifications admissions system.

R11 • Integrate careers services into academic affairs;
     • Review provision of careers guidance;
     • Integrate careers advice for lifelong learning.

R12 Review services offered to their students, in particular to meet the needs of part-time students.

R13 Develop/access teacher training programmes for staff and seek national accreditation from the ILTHE.

R14 Establish a professional Institute for Learning and Teaching in Higher Education.

R15 Development/promotion of computer-based learning materials, including kitemarking.

R16   Institutions to review programmes – breadth/depth.

R17   Develop admission procedures to emphasise key skills.

R18   Increase opportunities for work experience and reflection in programmes.

R19   Encourage employers to offer work experience for students.

R20   Institutions to develop Progress Files.

R21   Institutions to develop programme specifications, including outcomes in terms of knowledge, understanding and skills.

R22   Advantageous to have a national higher education qualifications framework.

R23   Specify criteria for franchising arrangements, and ensure compliance. Review current arrangements.

R24   Amend QAA remit (public information/standards verification/qualifications framework) and encompass arrangements in code of practice as condition of funding.

R25   Work on benchmark information on standards, recognised external examiners, develop complaints system, review degree status.

R26   Board of QAA to include a student and an international member.

R27   FBs, through the JISC, to continue to manage and fund C&IT services for researchers. In due course charges to be introduced based on usage.

R28   JISC to report on options to provide sufficient protected international bandwidth to support UK research.

R29   To establish Arts and Humanities Research Council (AHRC).

R30   Companies to take a strategic view of their relationship with higher education.

R31   Postgraduate research training to include the development of professional skills, e.g. communication, self-management and planning.

R32   To commission an evaluation of the funding of interdisciplinary research.

R33   All RAE panels to include one or more international members.

R34
- Research Council projects and programmes to meet full indirect costs and the costs of premises and central computing.
- To amend next RAE to encourage institutions to make strategic decisions about whether to enter departments or seek non-competitive funding.
- To establish an Industrial Partnership Development Fund to attract matching funds from industry, and assist regional and economic development.
- To establish a revolving public/private loan fund of £400 to £500m to support infrastructure in limited number of top quality research departments.

R35   To establish an independent body to advise Govt. on policy for public funding of research.

R36
- HEIs should be represented on regional bodies established by Govt.
- Further Education Funding Council should include a member from higher education

R37   Continue funding after April 1998 (HERDF) to support projects which enable higher education to be responsive to local industry and commerce.

R38   HEIs and industry to look at ways of giving firms access to information about HE services in their region.

R39
- Equity funding to support members of staff or students in taking forward business ideas developed in the institution;
- More technology incubator units.

R40   Encouraging entrepreneurship with innovative approaches to programme design and specialist postgraduate programmes.

R41   All HEIs to have institutional communications and information strategies.

R42   Managers appointed with both senior management experience and understanding of IT.

R43   Existing copyright legislation to be reviewed.

R44   To secure appropriate network connections to higher education and further education sites.

R45   Negotiate reduced tariffs from telecom providers for students.

R46   • Students to have access to a Networked Desktop Computer.
       • All students required to have own portable computer.

R47   Review staff development policies, make them available to all staff and consider Investors in People status.

R48   New full-time academic staff with teaching responsibility to achieve at least associate membership of Institute for Learning and Teaching.

R49   All institutions to maintain equal opportunities policies and publish progress on equal opportunities for all groups.

R50   Independent review committee to be appointed to report on framework for determining pay and conditions of service.

R51   Superannuation arrangements for academic staff to be harmonised, all new entrants to the USS.

R52   Develop arrangements for staff and external bodies to access and understand true costs of research.

R53   Review functions of Universities and Colleges Information Systems Association.

R54   Clarify position of HEI governing bodies.

R55   Action to ensure:
       • individuals may not serve as members of governing bodies for more than two terms, unless they also hold office;
       • governing body must include student and staff membership and majority of lay members;
       • an individual may not chair a governing body for more than two terms of office.

R56   Revise procedures to enable quick response (within 1 year) to an HEI requesting a change in size of governing body.

R57   Each governing body should review its effectiveness and the institution's performance once every five years.

R58   Performance indicators and benchmarks to be developed to assist in these reviews.

R59   As a condition of funding HEIs to publish annual reports on outcomes of reviews.

R60   Review arrangements for handling complaints from students.

R61   Funding arrangements should reflect diversity of institutional mission.

R62   Government should end the scope for confusion between title and name used by institutions.

R63   No change to the criteria for university status in medium term; in future there should be a period of relative stability in the number of universities.

R64   Measures to enable removal of degree-awarding powers where QAA has evidence of abuse of powers.

R65   To restrict use of the title 'University College'.

R66   Responsibility for decisions to establish new universities should be clarified and criteria developed.

R67   Priority in growth in sub-degree provision should be accorded to further education colleges. Higher education provision in further education should be funded directly and there should be no growth in degree level qualifications offered by further education colleges.

R68   To review mainstream teaching and research funding to ensure that collaboration is not discouraged. To bring forward annual allocations to support collaboration.

R69   QAA should ensure that its arrangements do not discourage collaboration.

R70   Annual review of total level of support for student living costs.

R71   Public spending on higher education should increase with the growth in GDP.

R72   Shift balance of funding from block grant towards a system in which funding follows the student.

R73 Public funding for HEIs should be determined on a rolling 3-year basis.

R74 Variations in the level of public funding for teaching should occur in special circumstances.

R75 To consider setting aside public funds to establish revolving loan schemes for several purposes, including:
- projects for refurbishment and maintenance of buildings;
- expensive (research or teaching) equipment purchases;
- collaborative projects to enable access to research (or teaching) facilities.

R76
- Waive tuition fees for part-time students in receipt of Jobseeker's Allowance;
- Review interaction between benefit entitlement and part-time study;
- Extend eligibility for Access Fund payments to part-time students.

R77 Arrangements for the equitable support of students of dance, drama and stage management.

R78 Introduction of income contingent terms for the repayment of student loans.

R79 Graduates in work to make a flat rate contribution of 25 per cent of the average cost of higher education tuition.

R80 Alternative approaches to national accounting which do not treat the repayable part of loans in the same way as grants to students.

R81 Scottish students who have had only 1 year's education after statutory schooling should not make a tuition contribution for one of their years in higher education.

R82 Inland Revenue should be used as the principal route for collection of income contingent contributions from graduates.

R83 Establishment of a unified Student Support Agency with responsibility for:
- assessing eligibility of individuals for public support;

- administering graduate contributions;
- means testing and paying grants for students' living costs;
- making per capita tuition payments to institutions.

R84   The tradition of institutional separation from national and sub-national levels of government is firmly maintained; and extended to Northern Ireland.

R85   Identify information needed to better inform students about higher education opportunities.

R86   Higher Education Funding Bodies in England and Wales to be responsible for funding all provision defined as higher education.

R87   Responsibilities of HEFCE and the TTA to be reviewed in drawing up proposals for the role of a General Teaching Council.

R88   Review of higher education in 5 years' time and subsequently every 10 years.

R89   HEIs in Northern Ireland to enhance their regional role.

R90   Expansion of higher education places in Northern Ireland.

R91   Adoption of Dearing 16–19 option for entry to Northern Ireland universities.

R92   Review of funding for research in Northern Ireland.

R93   Establish Northern Ireland Tertiary Education Forum, Higher Education and Further Education Funding Councils.

Appendix III: the 'Dearing Compact'

Society and taxpayers, as represented by the Government, were seen to contribute:

- a fair proportion of public spending and national income to higher education;
- greater stability in the public funding and framework for higher education.

In return they would receive the benefits of:
- a highly skilled, adaptable workforce;
- research findings to underpin a knowledge-based economy;
- informed, flexible, effective citizens;
- a greater share of higher education costs met by individual beneficiaries.

Students and graduates would contribute:

- a greater financial contribution … to the costs of tuition and living costs (especially for those from richer backgrounds);
- time and effort applied to learning.

In return for:
- more chances to participate in a larger system;
- better information and guidance to inform choice;
- a high quality learning experience;
- a clear statement of learning outcomes;
- rigorously assured awards which have standing across the UK and overseas;
- fairer income contingent arrangements for making a financial contribution when in work;
- better support for part-time study;
- larger access funds.

Institutions should supply:
- collective commitment to rigorous assurance of quality and standards;
- new approaches to learning and teaching;
- continual search for more cost-effective approaches to the delivery of higher education;
- commitment to developing and supporting staff.

Their benefits should include:
- a new source of funding for teaching and the possibility of resumed expansion;
- new funding streams for research which recognise different purposes;
- greater recognition from society of the value of higher education;
- greater stability in funding.

Staff in higher education contribute:
- commitment to excellence;
- willingness to seek and adopt new ways of doing things.

They should receive in turn:
- greater recognition (financial and non-financial) of the value of all of their work, not just research;
- proper recognition of their profession;
- fairer pay.

Employers should contribute:
- more investment in training of employees;
- increased contribution to the infrastructure of research;
- more work experience opportunities for students;
- greater support for employees serving on institutions' governing bodies.

Their resulting benefits include:
- more highly educated people in the workforce;
- clearer understanding of what higher education is offering;
- more opportunities for collaborative working with higher education;
- better accessibility to higher education for small and medium sized enterprises;
- outcomes of research.

Finally, *families of students*, while making a possible contribution to costs, should benefit from:
- better higher education opportunities for their children;
- better, more flexible higher education opportunities for mature students.

(NCIHE, 1997: 283)